Dentist's Tax & Business Architecture™

DENTIST'S TAX & BUSINESS ARCHITECTURE™

WHERE DENTISTS FINALLY MASTER MONEY, TAXES, AND LEGACY

NORMAN DOTCH

DENTIST TAX PLAN
Master Money, Taxes & Legacy.

Dentist's Tax & Business Architecture™

Published by Gatekeeper Press
7853 Gunn Hwy., Suite 209
Tampa, FL 33626
www.gatekeeperpress.com

Library of Congress Control Number: 2025950656

ISBN (paperback): 9781662971358
eISBN: 9781662971365

CONTENTS

INTRODUCTION

Imagine that you've decided to build the house of your dreams. You have been saving up money for years and years, you've toiled away in your chosen profession, you've made sacrifices, and now you are ready for the big payoff.

You collect your earnings, you hire a construction company, and you task them to build like they've never built before. A few months later, they tell you it's time to see the results and you race over to see your masterpiece.

Except, it's not a masterpiece. In fact, it's the most boring looking home you've ever seen. It's just a square with one door in the front, a few windows in various places, and a roof. No arches, no frieze boards, no shingles, no trim. The whole thing is painted grey, inside and out, and every single interior room is the exact same size.

You explode with rage at the construction manager. You want to know why you hired him if he was just going to do the least amount of work possible and cost you so much money in the process. When you finally run out of steam, he simply shrugs his shoulders and says, "I was just doing my job. You probably should have hired an architect first."

Yes, of course, every beautiful home needs an architect to draw up the perfect plans that reflect your wants, your likes, and your goals for a house. But architects don't just work in real estate. You'll find them in many fields where professionals need something crafted for their specific needs, to put them in position to enjoy as much success as possible, and to handle the technical side of specific industries that most people just don't have the knowledge to sort out on their own.

If you're reading this book, you're a dentist. Every year when you file your taxes, you take all your receipts and expenses and everything else to your friendly neighborhood CPA and expect him to turn it into some sort of financial windfall that will have the IRS sending you a nice refund check that will start funding your next financial goal.

Except, that's not what CPAs do. They run the numbers, file the forms, and mail the envelope or hit SEND on the screen. Their knowledge about tax strategies and tax laws is extremely narrow because it has little-to-nothing to do with their line of work.

They're in the volume game. The more clients they can round up before April 15 each year, the nicer their yearly income is going to be. Which means that when you and every other dentist in your city are all desperately trying to file before the deadline, that CPA is going through your tax forms faster than kids through a bag of candy the minute they get home from the semi-annual cleaning. The only time you'll hear from them is if you're missing a form. Otherwise, it does not matter one iota to them if you're going to owe the IRS $100,000 or get $100,000 in a refund. They get paid either way.

Just like our friend from the beginning of this chapter, it's time to realize that you've been hiring the wrong professional to do the wrong job every year. You don't need a CPA taking care of your dental practice taxes. You need an architect; an architect who understands The Dentist's Tax Truths System.

AN OPEN LETTER TO THE READER

Dear Doctor,

In your office, you are the expert. You got there by investing in your education, gaining experience wherever you could, and learning from your mistakes so you don't keep repeating them. Hiring a CPA to try and find places where you can find tax breaks in your yearly IRS filing is a mistake that way too many make over and over again, and every time it's costing them more and more of their hard-earned money.

Paying your taxes should never feel like a desperate race to shove a list of documents and data files at a CPA that you talk to for 30 minutes a year. The IRS gives you 365 days every year to plan out how to structure your taxes to maximize your profitability and ensure that you propel that success to the next year, and every year after that. Your CPA thrives in those final few days before April 15 by looking at what you did over the past year. What you've been missing all this time is the architect who will look ahead to where you're hoping to go and give you the best possible plan of how to get there with as much of your own hard-earned money as possible.

In the pages of this book, you're going to learn things that no CPA has the knowledge to tell you.

1. How to build structures that protect your net income and W2 taxable income
2. How to use the same laws that giant corporations use to play less in taxes
3. How to create wealth (outside of your license) and build your legacy while you're still active as a dentist.

These three combine to form The Dentist's Tax Truths System; an intricate combination of inside knowledge that over time becomes the difference between you working to barely make ends meet and you working to leave whatever legacy you want.

You don't need to go back to school to get a finance degree for this book to work for you. All you need to do is learn how the system works for you, rather than against you. The IRS isn't some bogeyman waiting to pounce on your hard-earned wages when you let your guard down. Once you understand how it functions and how tax laws are built to help, not hinder business owners such as yourself, you'll realize just what you've been missing out on and how to start hanging onto what's always been rightfully yours.

Welcome to your new education, where dentists master taxes, money, and their legacies. Welcome to The Dentist's Tax Truths System

Yours, Norman Dotch, RIA — The Dentist's Tax & Business Architect™

HOW THIS BOOK WORKS

If you were going to write a book about dental hygiene for the average person, you wouldn't use the scientific names of each tooth or go into heavy-duty analysis of how to perform complicated surgical procedures.

Similarly, this book is not going to take you step by step through every line of your tax return. What it is going to do is give you the best, most relevant information on how to:

- Identify and understand tax laws and codes that directly benefit dentists
- Create a year-long plan for handling your taxes so you're not desperately grasping at straws at 11:59 p.m. on December 31.
- Understand the way forward to continued tax success in your career

CHAPTER 1

The W2 or 1099 Associate Dentist

"Anytime is a good time to start a company" - Ron Conway

The Case Study: Dr. Melissa Hines decided to splurge about a month after getting her first job out of dental school, buying herself a steel blue Camaro to jet around town in. Why not? She had gotten on as an associate dentist in a practice just a few miles from the house she had grown up in. All of those long commutes to the city for dental school, all the late hours, all the debt incurred had finally paid off with her graduation and her first job. Sure, her client list wasn't that long, but she was doing actual work and getting paid for it. Plus, she was just a contractor, which meant very few responsibilities other than showing up for work every day. Let Dr. Taylor worry about all the headaches of running the practice. She was just here to get some experience, start knocking down her debt, and have some fun. Her dad even said he would keep doing her taxes for her like he had during medical school, so that was another headache out of the way.

The Reality: The minute Dr. Hines filled out that 1099-MISC form on her first day working for Dr. Taylor, whether she knew it or not, she officially became a business entity in the eyes of the

IRS. That might sound a bit frightening when you're straight out of dental school, but it should be the exact opposite. The US government loves when people start businesses because it generates local income and keeps that income in the US instead of watching it leave the borders. When Dr. Hines charges a patient, both she and Dr. Taylor earn revenue from it, and the government gets some of that revenue in the form of taxes. The government is grateful for people who maintain their businesses and thus make owning a business a privilege that allows you to get certain tax breaks when it's time to pay the IRS each year.

The Tax Code: IRS Code § 162 - Ordinary and Necessary Business Expenses: Allows any expense that is ordinary and necessary in your trade or business to be deducted.

What It Means: Dr. Hines isn't some random person, she's a small business owner, so she needs to act like one. She can start by creating an **entity**, which can be named as simply as her first and last names, a comma, and "DDS". More on the right entity in a minute. She can also open a **business checking account** from just about any bank in town. They'll love to have her as a client, and they'll show that love by offering her little perks for the new account. Plus, when she eventually decides to branch out on her own, she'll already have a relationship with a bank as a business client.

Next, Dr. Hines can start buying things she needs to be a proper dentist. Dr. Taylor should be providing her with all the basics, but what if Dr. Hines has a particular type of safety equipment, a brand of gloves, or something else that she got to use at dental school that Dr. Taylor doesn't offer? Sure, she could ask him to buy it, but she could also buy it herself, save the receipts, and **deduct the cost** of each thing from what she owes in taxes this year.

It's not a one-time deduction, either. She can keep track of how much each thing she buys depreciates over time and keep writing it off year after year until it hits its terminal point.

What Entity to Choose?

Dr. Hines is just one person, so she doesn't need to get fancy with how she sets herself up as a business entity. The most popular forms for individuals are:

- **S-Corporation:** If you're in business alone and your 1099 income exceeds $100,000.
- **LLC:** You're in business alone and you don't exactly know what your future plans are.

The S-Corporation can be appealing for Dr. Hines if she had a six-figure income. Let's say Dr. Taylor signs her to a $180,000 associate contract. That's a nice chunk of change other than the fact that she also has $300,000 in debt from dental school. If she forms an S-Corp, she can dictate how much of her income is paid to herself as a salary and how much is paid into distributions. Distributions are payments you take later to pay for expenses like your taxes and your health insurance, along with the cost of doing business. Dr. Hines could structure her business so that she pays herself a salary of $100,000 and takes the other $80,000 in distributions. For someone already so far in debt, she wants to pay as little in taxes as possible. In this scenario, she doesn't pay taxes on that $80,000 and saves $8,900 in FICA taxes next April 15.

What Can the Dental Business Entity Write Off?

There are an impressive amount of things you can spend money on and write off later on your taxes. All it takes is understanding what categories qualify, knowing how to keep your records, and remembering that anything physical holds value over an extended period of time - we call this depreciation. The following list includes the tax codes for several relevant items. Do not be intimidated by these numbers! They are included so that you can easily look up the codes on your own time to ensure that what you want to write off does qualify. Part of The Dentist's Tax Truths System is becoming comfortable with the basics of tax law and tax codes. This barrier keeps so many people from taking control of their own financial destiny.

- 1. Continuing Education & Licensing (§ 162)
- 2. Professional Insurance & Malpractice
- **3. Equipment & Supplies (§ 179 expensing)**
- 4. Business Travel (§ 274)
- 5. Home Office Deduction (§ 280A(c))
- 6. Health Insurance Premiums (§ 162(l))
- 7. Retirement Plan Contributions (§ 401(a))

The Tax Code: IRS Code § 179 - Depreciation Deduction for Business Assets: *Allows up to $1,220,000 in 2025 for qualifying equipment placed in service that year.*

What It Means: Yes, that is a whole lot of zeroes. This part of the tax code means that any equipment that you absolutely use in your practice, tallying all thc way up to $1.22 million this year, is something you can write off if you put it into service before December 31 of the current year. For a first-year dentist, that is probably way more than you are planning on spending, but it does mean that if you do have your eye on a piece of equipment - from a chair to digital scanner to a handpiece - buy it, and then watch it knock down your tax bill significantly.

CHAPTER 2

Entity Foundation

"The way to get started is to quit talking and begin doing."
– Walt Disney

The Case Study: Dr. Hines is getting ready to start her own practice after a couple of years working for Dr. Taylor, who has turned into both a mentor and a friend. Dr. Taylor tells Dr. Hines that a great idea would be to move from her existing S-Corporation that she used while in his service to a Corporation. It will open up a lot of avenues for her and give her a lot of options as she begins to expand. When Dr. Hines tells her CPA about it, he noticeably bristles, saying if she does that, he's going to have to redo her entire return, which he is nearly finished with already, even though she hasn't even technically hired him for the year yet. She hired the CPA for the first time a year ago when the tax bill was ridiculously high after her dad just ran it through TurboTax like always. The CPA saved her more money than Dad did, but still kind of felt like she was paying too much. The CPA had great reviews on Yelp, but she doesn't like feeling like she's getting a lecture, especially when she's the one paying the guy.

The Reality: A CPA wants you to stay the same every single year, because that makes it that much easier for them to auto-fill most of your tax return from last year's return and just plug in a few different numbers. Again, remember, their job is not to get you the best outcome on your taxes, just to file them for you. But changing from one entity structure to another is a perfectly logical thing to do as you start to move from one business plan to another. The following chart gives you a brief breakdown of four different entity types and what some of their pros and cons are.

Entity Type	Best Use	Tax Treatment	Key Benefits	Watch Out For
S-Corp	Solo/small group practice	Pass-through	Avoids SE tax on distributions	Must pay reasonable "salary"/ payroll admin
C-Corp	Income shifting @ lower 21% flat rate	Double taxed unless corporate loans	Fringe benefits, captive eligible	Corporate tax rate and formalities
LLC/ PLLC	Associate dentist start-ups or shared ventures	Pass-through	Simplicity, liability protection	SE tax on all income if no S-Corp election
Management Company (C-Corp)	Owns brand, leases equipment, employs staff	Separate return	Can prepaid expenses & own 831 (b)	Must set arm's length fees (3-5% of revenue)

The Tax Code: IRS Code § 351 — Transfer to Corporation Controlled by Transferor:

Permits tax-free transfer of property to a corporation in exchange for its stock, when the transferor controls at least 80 % after the exchange.

What It Means: Dr. Taylor isn't blowing smoke at Dr. Hines, he's doing her a great service. If she incorporates her dental practice and is the owner of at least 80% of its shares, she can roll her assets into it without having to pay taxes on them. A big part of the The Dentist's Tax Truths System is that you are going to move from one phase to another over the course of your career as your needs and goals change. Don't be scared of it. It's part of the successful path.

CHAPTER 3

From Associate to Practice Owner, Transition + Protection

"The avoidance of taxes is the only intellectual pursuit that still carries any reward." – John Maynard Keynes

The Case Study: Dr. Hines has made the big switch from being 'just' a dentist to the owner of a dental practice. But she isn't feeling great about the choice this morning. Her CPA sent her a draft of her tax return, and she just about hit the roof. She figured she would pay more this year now that she's a business owner and her profits have skyrocketed, the number he texted her is absolutely insane. She will pay it because she has to; the IRS has made plenty of famous examples of what it does to people who don't feel like paying a tax bill, but it's so large that she is going to have to stall out some plans for expansion ideas for next year.

The Reality: Owning a dental practice changes everything. You're no longer just a dentist; you're the person in charge. The buck stops here. Every decision is ultimately your decision. For the IRS, you're no longer just a provider of a service, you're a micro-enterprise; you're dealing with vendors, you're employing other people, you've got payroll, benefits, all the good stuff. Now you've got decisions to make about things like your tax strategy, your liability, and your cash flow. Every single thing you make a decision on has a ramification for how much money you keep at the end of the year. But one of the most important parts of The Dentist's Tax Truths System is to remember that you have 365 days to prepare and pay your taxes. April 15 is not the only day of the year that this can happen; it's the last possible day that too many people see as their last gasp effort.

IRS Code § 162 — Ordinary and Necessary Business Expenses: *If an expense keeps your business running, it's likely deductible—when documented and ordinary in dentistry.*

What It Means: Dr. Hines has all sorts of business expenses, and most of them are deductible. She needs to know exactly what is and what isn't now that she's the business owner. Because the truth is that dentists don't make more money by owning a practice. What separates the successful from the ones who just continue to tread water is the smart ones keep more of their money through planning. If you don't have a sound tax architecture in place, every additional dollar that you produce is going to be another dollar that is going to get taxed.

The Controlled Group Architecture

Once a dentist becomes an owner, they will have both clinical and administrative functions. This means further options on how to structure their business. Dentists who operate from a single entity blend risk and taxes into the same bucket. Two entities (MSO + PC) equal two buckets: one to protect assets, one to optimize deduction.

Entity Type	Best Use	Tax Treatment	Key Benefits	Watch Out For
Professional Corporation (PC)	Performs clinical dentistry	Dentist 100%	Pass-through or C-Corp	Qualifies for dental licensing
Management Services Organization (MSO)	Handles admin, marketing, HR, billing	Dentist via holding LLC or C-Corp	Separate return	Allows prepaid expenses, risk mitigation
831 (b) Captive	Insure risks of PC & MSO	Owned by MSO (C-Corp)	Pays tax only on investment income	Deductible premiums = retained wealth

The Risk Protection Blueprint

Insurance is a big part of being a business owner. Assuming something isn't likely to happen is as big a risk as anything you're going to see on this list. What would you rather have happen: Pay every month for something that never happens or never pay and have something happen that is 100% yours to pay for no matter how much it winds up closing? The good news is that the IRS allows dentists to manage risk pre-tax. That means you're not paying taxes on any policies or premiums you purchase, as long as you do it before the loss happens. For instance, Dr. Hines lives in Southeast Houston. That usually means no blizzards or tornados, but it puts her business in a direct line of fire for the hurricanes that hit the Gulf Coast of Texas every 8-10 years. If she decides to scrimp on natural disaster insurance because the hurricanes are so infrequent, she might save some money, but what about when one picks up speed over a couple of days, changes its course as they are often wont to do, and smashes right into her nice new building, causing catastrophic damage in the form of wind and floodwaters? There's no retroactive buying of tax-free insurance premiums after the storm has come and gone.

Risk	Entity	Shield	Tax Tie-In
Malpractice	PC only	Prof. insurance	Deductible (§ 162)
Admin errors/ employment	MSO	General liability	Deductible
Catastrophic events	831 (b) Captive	Internal insurance	Deductible premium / tax-deferred growth
Key-person loss	MSO	Key-Man policy (§ 101)	Tax-free death benefits; policy loan liquidity

CHAPTER 4

Liquidity, Leverage, Legacy - The Wealth Multiplier

"Investing is the key to building wealth." – Bola Sokunbi

The Case Study: Dr. Hines feels like she's running around with her hair on fire most days. She loves being her own boss and loves that she's building a steady stream of regular patients, but she's already worried about what her long-term plan looks like. When she has a good month, she's just sticking her profits in a savings account in the bank where they sit making an extremely low rate of interest until she invariably dips into them when she wants to buy something. It's not a good strategy, and she knows it. Last time she spoke to her CPA, she asked what sort of ways she could invest her money, and he said "probably a 401(k), but didn't elaborate. She has to stop asking that guy for his advice and remember he's just there to file her taxes for her. Her new way of thinking has to line up with The Dentist's Tax Truths System or she's going to fall short of all of her goals.

The Reality: Just like the IRS wants you to own a business, it also wants you to be able to save your money for later so that when you're done working, you can be independent. Every person that is self-reliant in their later years is one less person the government has to take care of. In addition, the government likes rewarding people who are smart with their money. The more you invest now, the better it is for everyone. There are five tax-free accounts that a dentist can put money into and enjoy massive benefits from down the road. These accounts all create liquidity that you can access later, and without the government coming with their hand out requiring their shares of taxes. You don't need Wall Street insider knowledge to build a wealth legacy, you need structure. All of these accounts are buckets where you can put money in for future tax-free wealth. The real trick is knowing which bucket you should fill first.

Account	IRS Section	Key Benefit	Annual Limits	Ideal For
Solo 401 (k)	§ 401(a) & § 402(g)	Large deductions & tax deferred growth	$69 000 (+$7,500 catch-up)	Self-employed dentists
ROTH 401(k)	§ 402A	Tax-free withdrawals at retirement	Same limits as 401(k)	Younger dentists expecting growth
HSA	§ 223	Triple tax advantage (pretax in, tax-free out for health)	$4 300 / $8 550 family	Dentists with HDHP
CESA (Education Savings)	§ 530	Tax-free education withdrawals	$2 000 per child /yr	Kids' college fund
GOLDEN Account	§ 408A Hybrid	Post-tax cash flow vehicle for late-career dentists Flexible	Flexible	Bridge to legacy and trust funding

Utilizing Whole Life Insurance

The Tax Code: IRS Code § 162 — Life Insurance Contracts Defined: *A 162 Executive Bonus plan allows a business to provide life and/or disability income insurance to key executives using tax deductible dollars.*

What It Means: If a policy meets the IRS definition of life insurance, its cash value grows tax-deferred and can be accessed tax-free via loans. A life insurance policy can be your best friend throughout the course of your career and beyond because it allows you to borrow money from an account that is constantly earning interest. The interest earned is greater than the percentage you are borrowing at, which means that the entire cash value continues to compound while you're paying back the loan.

Key features of a whole insurance policy

- Permanent coverage + guaranteed cash value.
- Mutual participating companies (OneAmerica, New York Life, Mass Mutual, Northwestern) have been paying nontaxable dividends for more than 150 years.
- Policy loans allow you to use the insurer's money while yours continues to earn

If Dr. Hines, (40 years old), signs up for a premium of $50,000 a year for the next 20 years, then her basis is $1,000,000. The guaranteed interest rate plus dividends (when declared and paid) it earns over the next two decades has a projected cash value of $1,323,607 at age

60. After 10 years or at age 70, with no additional contributions, the same as above, over the next decade has a projected cash value of $2,052,456, 100% tax free as a Supplemental Retirement Income. Let's say she wants to take out a $100,000 loan to do a total upgrade of office equipment. She does so at an arm's length. The $100,000 doesn't disappear from her account while she's borrowing it, she's borrowing it from the insurance company's general fund. Which means that over the 18 months that she's paying back the $100,000 plus interest, the same $100,000 is still in her account earning guaranteed rate plus dividends. Although the primary purpose of Whole life insurance is the death benefit (to protect loved ones), to build wealth, whole life insurance has nothing to do with death, it's all about liquidity. It creates capital that you control without having to hit up a bank or spend your precious equity.

When you create an MSO (C-Corp), you can fund a whole life insurance policy for yourself in a very tax-efficient method.

- MSO pays premium as compensation (§ 162 Bonus Plan).
- Adds 30 % Gross-Up to cover personal tax impact.
- You report your income once; policy grows tax-free thereafter.
- Pair with Short-Term Rental (STR) activity (§ 469 Active Participation) to offset income and eliminate the tax from bonus.

Stacking § 162 Bonus Plans with § 469 STR activity is one of the best ways to turn taxable W-2 income into tax-free wealth growth.

Summary

The rich don't get rich by earning more, they get rich by learning how to reuse their money without getting taxed. Now you have that power too.

Stage	Action	Tax Treatment	Outcome
Liquidity	Build cash in policies and accounts	Tax-deferred (§ 7702, § 401)	Emergency fund & investment fuel
Leverage	Borrow against policies	Non-taxable loan	Invest without liquidating assets
Legacy	Fund trusts / family office	Estate-tax shield (§ 2031–2042)	Multigenerational impact

CHAPTER 5

The Passive Activity Losses Rule & Real Estate Integration

"Buy land, they're not making it anymore." - Mark Twain

The Tax Code: IRS Code § 469 — Passive Activity Loss Limitations: *A 162 Executive Bonus plan allows a business to provide life and/or disability income insurance to key executives using tax deductible dollars.*

What It Means: You can't use your losses from passive activities, like investing in real estate, to offset income from your active business unless you **materially participate** or the activity qualifies you as an exception.

Let's knock out a few key definitions here:

Active income: Your W-2 salary / earnings from the business you participate in, i.e. being a dentist / owning a dental practice.

Passive income: Rental income or investments in which you do not materially participate.

Material participation: You must work 500+ hours a year or meet other requirements set by the IRS in order to qualify.

I'm not telling you to become a real-estate agent. I know how busy you already are. But there are a couple of loopholes here. One is that your spouse can qualify as a **real estate professional** (REP from here on out). The second is that you can use the **Short-Term Rental (STR) exception** to make your real-estate losses active. Here's how it works:

Real Estate Professional (REP) Status: You or your spouse can be classified as a REP if you satisfy two criteria.

1. You spend 750 hours a year in real-estate activities and more time in those activities than any other trade.
2. You materially participate in the properties you own.

Now, even if you spent 750 hours in real-estate activities, which is about 94 8-hour days, it's unlikely you would be able to spend more time doing that than running your dental practice. But your spouse can spend those 750 hours (or more) making being a REP their main work activity.

The Case Study: It's 10 years down the line and Dr. Hines is happily married to her husband Greg. She has earned $600,000 this year from her S-Corp practice, and over the past decade, the two of them have bought four rental homes. Greg is the manager of those four properties and easily surpasses 750 hours a year in that line of work. By using a cost-segregation study, they are able to show $210,000 of paper losses for the real estate investments. This lowers her taxable income for the year from $600,000 to $390,000 and saves Dr. Hines $84,000 in taxes.

The Short-Term Rental (STR) Rule

But what if Dr. Hines isn't married and still wants to take advantage of the loophole? Then she can use the STR Rule. The

STR Rule states that as long as a property is never rented for more than 7 days at a time, it is not a rental activity under the verbiage of IRS Code § 469, it is an active business. This means that as long as Dr. Hines materially participates in the business for at least 100 hours a year (not even 2 hours a week), and keeps records of her logs and hours, she can use the STR to offset her active practice income. This is why so many people are obsessed with having AirBNB-type rentals. They are amazing tax shelters. STRs are the bridge between dentistry and real estate. They turn real-estate depreciation into a direct tax savings for your practice income and it's all completely legal.

Cost Segregation & Bonus Depreciation

The Tax Code: IRS Code § 469 — Depreciation and Bonus Depreciation

What It Means: You can accelerate the depreciation of a qualified property to deduct up to 100% of cost in Year One (before December 31, 2030). Every property is a miniature factory for depreciation. When you buy real estate, realize you are buying it for both tax flow and cash flow.

Property Lifespans:

- 5-Year Assets: Furniture, appliances, equipment
- 7-Year Assets: HVAC, flooring, cabinets
- 15-Year Assets: Land improvements, driveways, pools

Workflow:

1. Engage engineer for cost segregation study.

2. Reclassify assets → shorter lives.
3. Apply § 168(k) bonus depreciation.
4. Flow losses through STR to offset clinical income

When you pair the Executive Bonus Plan (§ 162) from the MSO with STR losses (§ 469), you are effectively creating a legal offset loophole for yourself. This is where architecture turns into art. You have created a masterpiece in which two unrelated IRS sections are working together to build long-term, tax-free wealth for you.

Step	Flow	Tax Result
1	MSO pays Executive Bonus + Gross-Up ($130,000)	Deductible corporate expense
2	Dentist reports income of $130,000	Taxable personally
3	STR loss ($130,000) via bonus depreciation	Offsets personal income
4	Net tax = $0 — policy funded with tax-free dollars	Best possible outcome

CHAPTER 6

Captive Insurance Companies & Risk Mitigation

"Risk comes from not knowing what you are doing." - Warren Buffett

The Tax Code: IRS Code § 831 (b) — Tax on Insurance Companies Other than Life Companies

What It Means: Small property and casualty insurers with less than $2.8 million of annual written premiums may elect to be taxed only on investment income. Their underwriting profits are tax free inside the **captive**.

A traditional insurance policy transfers the risks of your life / business to outside carriers.

A captive means that this function comes in-house, where you are the insurance company ensuring your own practice, collecting premiums, and keeping the profits when the claims are low.

In any circumstances, you pay for insurance every year. But in the captive model, you pay yourself first, and the IRS approves if you've structured it properly.

A captive must cover real insurable risks that are priced by an actuary who has no relationship with you or your family. If you try to pass off fake or implausible risks, you're going to get in trouble. A captive can be used to insure:

- Cyber liability & data breach
- Employee dishonesty & HR claims
- Regulatory & HIPAA penalties
- Key vendor failure / supply chain
- Business interruption
- Pandemic losses and marketing recovery

A captive is not a tax shelter, but a risk silo. Its tax advantages are a happy by-product of something that every business should already be doing: insure, reserve, and retain. The tax deduction benefits of a captive include:

1. Operating Unit: deducts premiums under § 162 (ordinary business expense).
2. Captive: pays no tax on underwriting profit, only on investment earnings.
3. Management Co.: Receives Captive dividends tax-free (§ 243 DRD – Dividends- Received Deduction).
4. Key-Man Funding: Mgmt. Co. uses dividends to fund Whole Life policy on the dentist (owner & beneficiary). Split-Dollar (Economic Benefit Regime).

In order to create your own captive, you'll need to ensure you have compliance and you do everything right to protect yourself from a future audit. To do so, you'll need to follow five requirements.

Requirement	Description
Actuarial Study	Annual pricing justified by independent actuary
Feasibility Report	Proves legitimate business purpose
Form 8886	Filed if IRS classifies transaction as reportable
Board Minutes	Record premium decisions & claim reviews
Arm's-Length Policies	Market-rate premiums and coverage terms

There are five common pitfalls to avoid when you create your own captive. The easiest way to not have to worry about them is to treat it like it's a real insurance policy - which it is - that just happens to also do well for you for tax purposes.

1. Unrealistic premiums or duplicate coverages
2. Loans or guarantees to your relatives
3. Personal use of captive assets
4. Failure to file Form 8886
5. Treating the captive policy as an investment vehicle and not an insurance policy.

When your captive matures, you have effectively created a private reserve bank that you are both owner and only customer of. It protects your practice today and grows your wealth and legacy for tomorrow by:

- Creating a permanent reserve of untaxed profits
- Reducing dependency on commercial insurers
- Strengthening balance sheets for credit and sale
- Allowing tax-favored funding for Whole Life and trusts

CHAPTER 7

Legacy & Trust Architecture

"Legacy is not something for people. It's leaving something in people."
- Peter Strople

The Case Study: With her years as a dentist almost up, and her children grown, moved out, and providing her with lots of grandchildren to dote on, Dr. Hines finds the topic of her legacy on her mind a lot. Her children will each inherit a lot of money when she passes from the Earth if she does things the simple way, but she's also reflecting a lot on how her life was impacted by others. She's considering leaving an endowment to the dental school that got her ready for the life to come and also wants to give back to a few charities that she was a volunteer with in her younger days that she knows could use contributions to help keep the doors open. But she's also heard horror stories of how people's money gets all mucked up after they pass if they don't have everything set up just right, so she knows she has to get prepared.

What it Means: Most dentists are laser focused on production, income, and assets. That's how they're paying the bills, keeping the doors open, and moving forward year by year. But the legacy you leave to the people you care about the most is a lot more than numbers after a dollar sign. It's about what your wealth means to you and whom you want it to serve. Without proper structure, your wealth is fragile and can be taken by entities you don't want anywhere near it. Without purpose, your wealth will have little meaning to those who wind up with it.

Legacy planning is the final pillar in your tax architecture, following Business, Personal, and Retirement.

The Tax Codes:

- § 671–679 — Grantor Trust rules
- § 2503 — Gift Tax Exclusions
- § 2055 — Charitable Estate Deductions
- § 1014 — Step-Up in Basis at Death

Trusts are like dental crowns. They are there to protect, preserve, and strengthen something that has already been built. If you don't have a trust structure in place by the time you're 45 years old, you're gambling with your own future and the financial future of the people you want to leave your legacy to. The following table lists six types of trusts to consider as you plan your legacy.

Core Legacy Instruments for Dentists

Structure	Purpose	Tax Advantage
Revocable Living Trust	Avoid probate, privacy	Step-up in basis, seamless transition
Irrevocable Life Insurance Trust (ILIT)	Hold Whole Life (§ 7702) outside estate	Death benefit estate-tax free
Grantor Retained Annuity Trust (GRAT)	Freeze asset value, transfer appreciation	Minimized gift tax
Charitable Remainder Trust (CRT)	Donate appreciated assets, retain income	Capital gains deferral + deduction
Family Limited Partnership (FLP)	Centralize family wealth management	Valuation discounts + control
Private Foundation or DAF	Charitable giving vehicle	Deduction up to 30 % of AGI

When you have a patient that needs dental restorations, you don't just have them open wide, crack your knuckles, and have them out the door an hour later. It takes planning and engineering of the highest order, overseen and operated by a master professional like yourself. Legacies are built the exact same way, they take time and dedication to preserve them across multiple generations.

The Controlled Group Legacy Model

Using this model results in no estate tax, no income tax, and no probate; only controlled, tax-free liquidity. This is how you maintain the goals of The Dentist's Tax Truths System.

Your Controlled Group — consisting of your Practice (PC or S-Corp), Management Company(C-Corp), Captive (831(b)), and Retirement Plan (Roth 401(k)) — can funnel wealth directly into your Family Office and trusts.

Here's how it all comes together:

1. Operating Entity (PC) pays management fees →
2. Management Company (C-Corp) receives fees → pays premiums to Captive (831(b))
3. Captive distributes dividends → Management Company →
4. Management Company funds Whole Life policy (§ 7702) →
5. Policy owned by Irrevocable Trust (ILIT) →
6. Trust loans or gifts to heirs, funds family foundation, or invests in real estate.

Family Governance

If you've ever had even a minor stake in someone's inheritance where there was confusion about how it was structured or what their will said, you know it is one of the most frustrating situations to be in, and that it can turn people from the same ugly into enemies very quickly. Therefore, a huge part of the architecture of your legacy should focus on **family governance**, that is teaching your heirs how to provide stewardship to your legacy.

Topics to be covered include:

- Family constitution (values, philanthropy goals).
- Annual family board meetings.
- Investment policy statements.
- Successor education (financial literacy & ethics).
- Trustee mentoring (gradual control transfer).

Leaving a Charitable Legacy

When you have wealth with a strong architecture around it, it can turn into a dynasty of giving. Without that strong architecture, the wealth by and large dies with the creator.

The Tax Codes: § 170, 2055 - Charitable Contribution Deductions: *Donations to qualified charities, DAFs, or private foundations are deductible within AGI limits.*

What It Means: There are three charitable tools for dentists to be aware of. Donor-Advised Funds (DAFs), which have the easiest entry and are front-loaded deductions.

Private Foundations: You have full control, and you fund causes that you choose.

Charitable Remainder Trusts (CRTs): You sell appreciated assets and retain the income.

The following table sums up the Legacy Integration Blueprint.

Pillar	Core Instrument	Tax Benefit
Business	Controlled Group (PC, Mgmt. Co., Captive, Roth)	Income & estate tax control
Personal	Whole Life (§ 7702)	Tax-free liquidity
Retirement	TAX PLANNING Roth 401(k)	Tax-free growth & Tax-free distribution
Legacy	ILIT, FLP, CRT	Estate elimination + multigenerational wealth

CHAPTER 8

Advanced § 7702 Strategies & Infinite Banking Mastery

"The Infinite Banking system is not just for the present - it builds a financial foundation that benefits future generations, emphasizing stewardship." - Jason Powers

The Tax Codes: § 7702 — Definition of Life Insurance Contracts

What it Means: For a policy to be treated as life insurance for tax purposes, it must pass one of two tests: the Cash Value Accumulation Test (CVAT) or the Guideline Premium and Corridor Test (GPT). If your policy passes, the cash value growth is tax-deferred, and the policy loans are tax free. Tax code § 7702 is exceedingly rare because it is one of just a few codes that allow your wealth to grow, distribute, and transfer without any of it touching your 1040. Remember your Whole Life policy is not an expense, it's a balance sheet asset that earns while you borrow.

How to Design Your Infinite Banking System in 5 Steps

Step 1: Establish a Whole Life Policy with Paid-Up Additions (PUAs).

Step 2: Fund policy from pre-tax sources where possible (Mgmt. Co. bonuses, Captive dividends).

Step 3: Access cash value via policy loans to buy assets in year one

Step 4: Let cash value keep compounding while you use the carrier's money.

Step 5: Repay loans strategically or allow death benefits to self-liquidate.

Dentists can use this for:

- Creating guaranteed growth and dividends
- Providing tax-free liquidity via policy loans
- Generating estate protection through a tax-free death benefit.

Weighing Executive Bonus vs. Economic Benefit Split-Dollar Strategies

Strategy	Entity Pays	Dentist Reports	Outcome
§ 162 Executive Bonus + Gross-Up	Management Company (C-Corp)	W-2 bonus income + tax gross-up	Creates policy owned by dentist personally
Split-Dollar (Economic Benefit)	Management Company owns policy	Dentist reports "economic benefit" (cost of insurance only)	Policy cash value grows off-balance sheet

Audit and Compliance Considerations

Rule	Requirement
§ 7702 Limits	Must stay below MEC threshold (Mod. Endowment Contract)
Documentation	Show bonuses or dividends funding policy were arm's length
Entity Ownership	If Split-Dollar, Mgmt. Co. must be owner & beneficiary
Loan Use	If for investment, track interest for deductibility § 163
Carrier Selection	Only mutual participating insurers (150+ yrs dividend history)

The Liquidity > Leverage > Legacy Cycle

- Liquidity — Fund Whole Life policy.
- Leverage — Borrow against cash value for investment / expansion.
- Legacy — At death, policy pays tax-free benefit to trust.

Remember, every dollar you run through Tax Code § 7702 goes to battle for you, the goals that you are pursuing, and the freedom and comfort you want your family to enjoy after you are gone.

CHAPTER 9

Controlled Groups, MSOs & Compliance Architecture

"Each new situation requires a new architecture." - Jean Nouvel

The Tax Codes:

- § 1563 – Controlled Groups of Corporations
- § 414(b)–(m) – Aggregation of Related Employers (retirement plan compliance)
- § 482 – Arm's-Length Transactions

What it Means: A Controlled Group consists of one or more corporations that are connected through common ownership or control. If you are the owner of these corporations, you can coordinate their deductions, their management fees, and their benefit plans across multiple entities. However, you must maintain compliance at all times and you must prove effective arm's length transactions.

You're great at doing surgery, right? How would you feel doing it with one hand tied behind your back? Sounds preposterous, right? Yet that's what you're doing if you're operating everything about your business inside a single entity like an S-Corp.

With a Controlled Group structure, you can separate your management income, your clinical income, your risk, and your retirement planning into specialized entries that each have their own strengths to lower your tax bill far more than they would all bunched together. In the Controlled Group model, each of the entities has a specific role and together they make beautiful music together. Your Controlled Group is the conductor that makes The Dentist's Tax Truths System a reality.

The Four-Entity Controlled Group Model

Entity	Type	Function	Tax Benefit
A — Dental Practice (PC / PLLC)	Professional Entity	Operates clinical services	Qualifies for § 199A deduction
B — Management Company (C-Corp)	Administrative Entity	Handles marketing, HR, billing, compliance	Prepay expenses; choose fiscal year
C — Captive Insurance (831(b))	Risk Entity	Insures practice specific risks	Deductible premiums; tax-deferred growth
Self-Directed SOLO 401(k) / SOLO ROTH 401(k)	Retirement Entity	Greater Control, Higher Contribution, Alternative Investment	Tax-free growth/ Taxed as ordinary income/tax-free distribution

The Management Services Organization (MSO)

A dentist has to separate their clinical ownership from their management operations in order to stay compliant. This is based on each state's corporate practice of medicine (CPOM) laws. That structure looks like this:

- **Dental PC/PLLC** — Provides patient care.
- **MSO (C-Corp)** — Provides business and administrative support.

- **MSO** charges the practice an arm's-length management fee (e.g., 3–5 % of revenue).

The IRS is not going to worry much about the structure you create as long as you document it. In the rare chance that you get audited, but you have all the documentation required to substantiate your claim, that's a golden ticket to the IRS. It means that not only do you understand what you're doing, but you realize how vital it is to document what you're doing.

Here are the five components you need to ensure are taken care of for compliance in your architecture.

- **Arm's-Length Transactions (§ 482):** All intercompany fees must reflect market value.
- **Unified Control (§ 1563):** Common ownership must be properly documented.
- **Retirement Aggregation (§ 414):** All employees across the group must be included for retirement plan compliance.
- **Captive Legitimacy (§ 831(b)):** Must insure real business risks with actuarial justification.
- **MSO Structure:** Must comply with state CPOM laws — MSO cannot dictate clinical decisions

Sample Documentation Blueprint

Document	Purpose
Operating Agreements	Define ownership, roles, and control
Management Services Agreement (MSA)	Specifies MSO duties, fees, and term
Captive Insurance Policies	Define risks and coverage scope
Arm's-Length Fee Analysis	Substantiates pricing between entities
Annual Board Minutes	Record of compliance and major decisions
Independent Valuations	Ensures fair market value consistency

Be aware that your C-Corp (MSO) can select a fiscal year with a different starting point from your calendar year PC. You can use this to create more flexibility in the timing of your income and your tax prepayments under tax code §461 and §446.

Remember, risk management is the only business that can turn into wealth for you. That's why smart dentists all own their own insurance companies.

Summary of Controlled Group Benefits

Benefit	Explanation
Tax Efficiency	Deductible management fees and premiums reduce taxable income
Asset Protection	Risk isolated in Captive + MSO
Retirement Leverage	Roth 401(k) grows tax-free
Legacy Control	Whole Life and Trust integration
Operational Flexibility	Fiscal year selection; prepayment of 12-month expenses
Audit Shielding	Fiscal year selection; prepayment of 12-month expenses

CHAPTER 10

The Secret to your Success: Help from a Tax Architect

"You don't pay taxes–they take taxes."–Chris Rock

Case Study: When Dr. Hines decided to go to dentistry school, she was still at a four-year college, living at home to save money, and her parents still had her on their health insurance, auto insurance, and were doing her taxes for her when she had enough income to warrant filing. When she was under 25 years old, they could keep her on their insurance without incurring any penalties and it was a lot less expensive than her paying for it on her own. But as we saw in Chapter 1, when she got that first job as associate dentist, her dad paid her taxes for her and she paid way more than she should have because all he did was use Turbo Tax and plug in some numbers.

In their second year, she knew she was going to need professional help, and after looking around on Google decided to hire a CPA to do her taxes for her. She saved some money compared to when her dad did her taxes, but it wasn't some overwhelming difference between one and the other. As she starts to consider going into business for herself, she's fearful that her tax bills will skyrocket as her earnings and as assets do.

What It Means: When Dr. Hines is an associate dentist working on a contract for a dental practice owner, we consider her in need of **Level I Tax Architecture**. Dr. Hines is either working off a W-2 or a 1099, but she can and should still operate as a business entity because it allows her to write off deductions throughout the year. The average CPA isn't going to bother telling a client any of those things because it is not part of their job description. Dr. Hines doesn't need to try and rely on a CPA however. She can instead subscribe to the Tax Truths Tax Planning Software & Learning Academy for Dentists. This LMS software package provides dentists with a step-by-step guide through the specific IRS codes (IRCs) and sections that can help them buid their businesses from a mere paycheck into a small company that is entitled to numerous tax breaks. The LMS can be customized to fit every dentist's specific needs, starting with a Tax Risk Assessment, which allows them to input all of their relevant data and figure out where they are missing out on opportunities to save. From there, it builds a customized tax plan that is constructed to help protect up to 100% of her annual taxable income.

As she moves into owning her own practice, Dr. Hines' world expands enormously and she can no longer rely solely on someone whose job is largely to be a bookkeeper to handle her custom needs. She still needs her relationship with her parents, but it's going to change from total reliance to specific levels of support. The same is true with her relationship with her CPA.

Leveling Up

When she starts moving towards her own practice and starting to think about saving for retirement and building a legacy, her needs expand to **Level II** Tax Architecture. As you can see in the graphic below, she is now greatly expanding her scope of influence to now only include her own personal earning as a dentist. Dr. Hines is moving from the realm of the LLC and the S-Corp towards a C-Corp where she has numerous expenses, which also means numerous deductions. She's considering how to start saving for retirement through Solo and Roth 401(k) plans, and as she gets closer to the middle of life, she's also taking steps to secure the legacy she wants to leave for her descendants and the special people in her life. She's functional in four pillars now, seeking:

- **Create in her Personal** realm through the earnings she makes a business
- **Keep in her Business** realm through using the correct business entities to maximize the amount of money she keeps at the end of the year.
- **Multiply in her Retirement** realm by taking smart steps that reduce her tax load now and in the future.
- **Impact in her Legacy** realm by making administrative moves now that keep the IRS and non-welcome participants out of the inheritance she will someday leave behind.

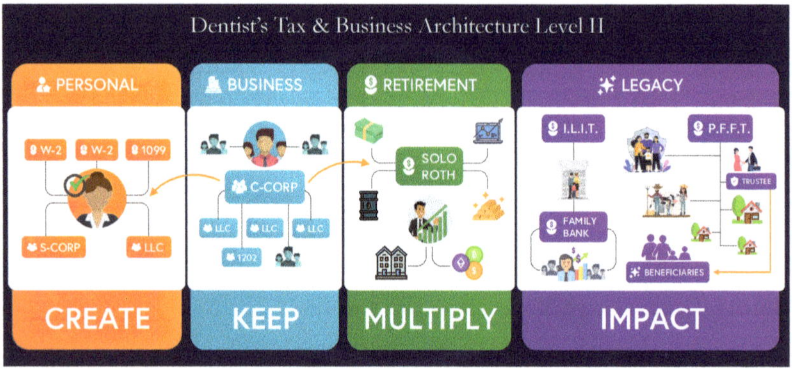

Of course, Dr. Hines isn't going to stop there. Every stop on her journey onwards and upwards gets her a little closer to the point where she steps away from the practice and basks in the glow of retirement where everyday is an opportunity to do something she loves without having to worry about any financial constraints whatsoever

As she has children, she'll want to add education investment accounts to her portfolio. As she becomes a powerhouse of a dental practice owner, she might wind up owning multiple practices, or creating her own insurance captive for dual purposes, or investing in real estate as another way to house money and keep it safe from the IRS over the long run. What we start to really see is that Dr. Hines is no longer just a dentist, no longer just a business owner. She has created her own financial empire; an amazing, diverse series of holdings, accounts, assets, and investments that are all designed to do one thing: provide for her dreams in the future and her legacy beyond the end of her mortal days. She has advanced to the need for **Level III** Tax Architecture. She has gone from helping just the person in the dentist's chair to helping every single person. Every step she takes is a step closer to those dreams but also takes more of a guiding hand to ensure everything is running smoothly.

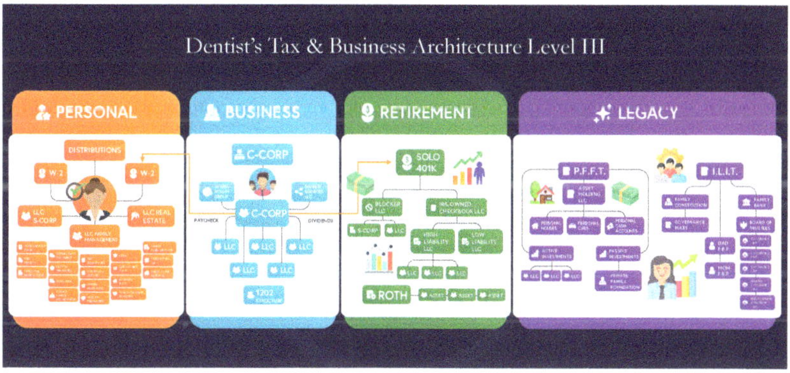

As her practice expands so does her earning potential. Dr. Hines will find the LMS still a great help, but as things grow more complex, the need for human assistance will become paramount. She's upgrading her practice and every facet of her finances, so it's time to upgrade to a tax architect. A tax architect is a specialist who will use the techniques found in the LMS and expand them to where every day of the year is an opportunity for the dentist to save money on taxes, structure her assets, and put structures in place to protect her profits now and turn them into tax-free investments that stretch far into the future. Tax architects study tax law as a full-time professional and work with their clients to take a career and turn it into a lifetime of financial success. They do all of the heavy lifting on creating a workflow and an architecture that shields a dentist's profits from the IRS by using every possible tax code and vehicle to put your money in places where it stays with you over the long-term. Tax architects build for the future, meaning the dollars you are making now become powerful investment tools that grow and grow to provide comfort and sustainability for your retirement years or your legacy. This is not a job for a lawyer, a bookkeeper, or a CPA. The tax architect is a unique professional capable of helping the smart dentist create wealth and lower their tax liability enormously.

When you hire a tax architect, the IRS goes from being your biggest fear to becoming your biggest ally.

Never be afraid to grow larger in your dental practice. Never be afraid to dream bigger. You are a rare breed of professionals who provide a service and a level of comfort that few others can. You should be rewarded for your service because of your level of care, your level of education, and the hard work you have put into it to get to this point.

CHAPTER 11

The Dentist's Family Office Blueprint (VFO)

"If you're going to establish a system aimed at spanning generations, you have to be willing to evolve." - Ennino Mercuri

A **Family Office** refers to a private organization that is dedicated to managing the wealth, investments, and legacy of a single family: YOURS. While this used to be the playground of extremely high-net-worth families $100m or more, there are new tools in place that allow dentists earning between $1.0-$1.5 million per year to build a **Virtual Family Office** (VFO) structure with the same types of benefits. This is about teamwork. This is the heart of The Dentist's Tax Truths System. If your CPA, tax attorney, and tax advisor aren't in communication with each other on a regular basis, you don't have a team, but a group of individuals who only care about themselves, not you and your goals.

The Dentist's Family Office Framework

Pillar	Function	Professionals
Tax Architecture	Proactive strategy, compliance, IRS defense	Tax Architect, CPA
Investment Architecture	Active + alternative investments	RIA, Real Estate Advisor
Insurance Architecture	Risk management, § 7702 planning	Advanced Insurance Planner
Legal Architecture	Entity, trust, and estate management	Tax Attorney, Estate Counsel
Philanthropy Architecture	Foundations, DAFs, giving plans	Charitable Trust Specialist

All of these components can be integrated together under one unified **Wealth Dashboard** which is powered by **The Tax Truths Software + Academy**.

Core Components of the VFO

Each entity on this list plays a role in the VFO, which mirrors a corporate structure. It has been adapted and optimized and adapted here to fit your personal legacy.

Component	Description	Control Mechanism
Practice Entity (PC/ PLLC)	Operates and produces cash flow	Owns key contracts, pays MSO
MSO (C-Corp)	Central hub for management, payroll, benefits	Fiscal-year flexibility
Captive (831(b))	Risk management and tax deferral	Distributes dividends post 12 months
Roth 401(k)	Tax-free retirement growth	Tax-free retirement income
Trusts & Foundations	Preserve wealth, protect family	Control distributions, set governance

Building Your VFO Team

A true VFO isn't just a group of people, it's the right specialists who are doing specific roles under the guidance of an overall architect. Every wealthy family has a boardroom of advisors. Why shouldn't every successful dentist have the same?

- **The Tax Architect (Norman Dotch)** – Designs the structure and ensures tax code integration.
- **CPA (Compliance Specialist)** – Files under direction, not control.
- **Estate Attorney** – Drafts ILITs, GRATs, CRTs, FLPs, etc.
- **The Registered Investment Advisor (RIA) (Norman Dotch, RIA)** – Coordinates portfolio across taxable and tax-free accounts.
- **The Advanced Insurance Planner (Norman Dotch)** – Implements § 7702 and Tax Favored Invesment Strategies Such as §162 Executive Bonus + Gross Up Arrangements and Corproate Owned key-man (Split-Dollar Economic Benefit & Loan Regime) Policies
- **Bookkeeper** – Maintains documentation and entity books.
- **Philanthropy Officer (Optional)** – Oversees foundations and giving plans.

VFO Business Protocol

The VFO is a business, and thus it must always act like a business, including making sure the following are happening to appease the IRS and reduce the risk of an audit. Remember, the difference between a tax plan and a tax shelter is paperwork. One is a strategy that can save you millions. The other is sloppy work that can cost you your legacy. A VFO is the final form of tax mastery, where your money is checking in with scheduled reports to let you know how it is doing.

Compliance and Control

The Tax Codes:

- § 482 – Arm's-length inter-entity transactions
- § 1563 – Controlled Group definition
- § 831(b) – Captive taxation
- § 7702 – Life insurance definition
- § 414(b) – Retirement plan aggregation

Best Practices Checklist

1. Separate EINs for each entity
2. Annual board meetings with documented minutes
3. Inter-entity agreements for MSA, lease, and insurance
4. Captive feasibility studies
5. Annual valuations
6. Maintain "ordinary and necessary" standard under § 162

Professional Enterprise Checklist

1. Schedule quarterly review meetings just like a board of directors
2. Maintain a monthly management dashboard for KPIs and tax metrics
3. Document every inter-entity transaction and the reason for it
4. Provide annual "Family Report" summarizing growth, liquidity, and legacy updates

The VFO Control Dashboard

Powered by The Tax Truths Software, each dentist gains an integrated system where:

- Entity structures are mapped visually.
- Tax strategies are calculated and tracked (monthly savings).
- § 7702 loans, Roth accounts, and Captive balances are monitored.
- Documents (agreements, valuations, filings) are digitally archived.

This transforms your office into a living, breathing financial ecosystem

CHAPTER 12

The 2030 Vision & The Dentist Legacy Network

"The most reliable way to predict the future is to create it." - Abraham Lincoln

By 2030, our goal is to not just help as many dentists as possible save as much money in taxes as they can, but to establish a paradigm shift in the entire culture of dentistry that moves dentists from a state of relying on others to show them how to manage their finances to being strategic masters of their own practices and legacies. The IRS gives every dentist 365 days each year to plan their taxes. For some reason, your CPA makes you think everything happens in the two weeks before April 15.

Our goal has four key points to it:

1. Educate 10,000 dentists nationwide through The **Dentist Tax Truths Training Academy**.
2. Build **1,000 Dentist-Owned Family Offices (VFOs)** across the US
3. Establish **The Dentist Legacy Network** – a private professional community of dentists mastering money, taxes, and legacy together.
4. Protect **$10 billion** in wealth from unnecessary taxation by 12/31/2030 ("The Big Beautiful Bill" expiration).

Introducing the Dentist Legacy Network (DLN)

The DLN is a private membership community for all dentists who are part of the Tax Truths Software & Academy family. It is designed as the professional home for financially independent, tax literate dental professionals. It is bound by four essential pillars.

Pillar	Description	Access Level
Education	Continuous tax law training & updates	All members
Implementation	Guided software use & mentorship	Core/Pro subscribers
Collaboration	Peer case studies & success panels	Network events
Legacy Building	Generational wealth & philanthropy training	Elite members

Members will also participate in exclusive webinars, regional summits, and the annual Dentist Wealth Architects Conference.

The DLN Ecosystem

Component	Purpose	Tool
The Tax Truths Software & The Training Academy	Central data + Tax Code strategy Archive & Structured 12-week education system	$ / Monthly Subscription & Self-paced or live
Private Client Program	Implementation + Done-for-you tax architecture	$/year engagement
Legacy Network Community	Collaboration & mentorship	Exclusive online forum
Annual Summit	Optional in-person education & recognition	Keynote

The Dentist's Financial Evolution Path

The more you understand the tax codes, the less you'll pay the IRS. You should never think of this sort of education as an option. It is the armor that keeps your income, your family, and your legacy safe.

Stage	Dentist Type	Focus	Strategic Outcome
Level 1 — The Associate	1099 / W-2	Earning efficiently	Learn § 162, § 280A(g), § 199A
Level 2 — The Owner	Practice owner	Structuring wisely	Implement MSO, Captive, TAX PLANNING
Level 3 — The Architect	Advanced planner	Multiplying wealth	Master § 7702, § 469, § 831(b)
Level 4 — The Legacy Builder	Multi-entity owner	Perpetuating family wealth	VFO + Trust Architecture

The Final Transition: From Dentist to Architect

The day you graduated from your medical school you became a dentist.

The day you started making you, you became an entrepreneur.

Now you're a tax and business architect - and know more about the financial side of your profession than 99.9% of your peers.

By mastering the contents of this book, you have taken control of your own fate in dentistry and life by learning:

- How to make money intelligently
- How to multiply it strategically
- How to protect it legally

- How to pass it on meaningfully

True wealth is measured not in numbers, but in control: Control of our time, your taxes, and your future.

This is The Dentist's Tax Truths legacy.

FINAL THOUGHTS

Mastering Money, Taxes, and Legacy

"Intelligence solves problems and produces money. Money without financial intelligence is money soon gone." - Robert Kiyosaki

Your Journey Revisited

When you began reading this book, you were a dentist — trained to restore smiles, not balance sheets.

But now, you've learned that wealth is built with the same precision as dentistry itself: one structure at a time, one code at a time, one plan at a time.

You've discovered that tax law isn't an enemy to fear — it's a blueprint written for those who take the time to understand it.

The IRS didn't create loopholes. It created invitations — and the professionals who accept them are the ones who build true financial freedom. Once you master this concept, you'll wonder why every dentist isn't doing the same.

Why It Matters

Dentistry is one of the most demanding professions in America. You are dealing with patients of every single type, with a wide range of habits, needs, pain thresholds, you name it.

You heal others at the cost of your own time, energy, and sometimes even your peace of mind.

You deserve more than a reactive accountant who files after the year ends and vanishes for the next 11 months.

You deserve an Architect.

Someone who builds.

That is the heart of The Dentist's Tax Truths.

Not just to teach you how to save on your taxes, but to help you understand why you overpay them and how to finally take control of your own legacy.

From Compliance to Control

Every year, the IRS gives you 365 opportunities to plan.

Your CPA only takes one — April 15. Then he or she stops thinking about you until next April 14.

But when you learn to think like an architect, every day becomes an opportunity to move a dollar from "taxable" to "protected."

The difference between the dentist who retires broke and the one who retires wealthy isn't income.

It's all about initiative.

Those who wait for advice will always be taxed.

Those who design their own architecture will always lead.

The Role of Your CPA

Let's be clear — your CPA isn't the villain.

They have their role: compliance and filing.

But your CPA's job ends where your Tax Architect's job begins.

You still need them — but you lead them.

When your CPA says, "I've never heard of that,"

your response should be: "That's because you've never planned like an architect."

Never feel intimidated to ask questions or challenge someone who files your taxes. Remember, you're the one paying them.

What Comes Next

This book is your education. Your next step is implementation.

You've learned how to:

- Structure your entities correctly (LLC, S-Corp, C-Corp, MSO, Captive).
- Use your retirement plan as an investment engine (TAX PLANNING + Roth 401(k)).
- Multiply money through § 7702 Whole Life and Infinite Banking.
- Integrate real estate, trusts, and charitable strategies.
- Build your own Virtual Family Office.

Now it's time to put your education to work inside The Tax Truths Software and Training Academy.

This is where your plan stops being theory and starts becoming wealth.

The Invitation

Dentists across the country are joining the DLN — a movement of professionals who no longer let their CPAs dictate their destiny.

They plan early, act strategically, and use every day of the 365 the IRS gives them.

You are now one of them.

You've read the book.

You've seen the truth.

Now you have the tools.

Remember, tax law isn't about avoidance — it's about awareness. Awareness is the greatest financial freedom of all.

A Final Word from the Architect

People always ask me:

"Why Taxes? Why Dentists?"

My answer never changes:

Because both require precision, discipline, and a steady hand.

Two decades ago, I met a dentist who had nearly lost everything — his savings, his retirement, and his confidence.

By showing him how to use the tax code proactively, not reactively, he transformed his life in just five years.

He retired debt-free, built a legacy for his children, and told me,

"You didn't just save my money. You saved my future."

That conversation changed me.

And since that day, this mission hasn't been about numbers.

It's been about purpose — empowering professionals who deserve more.

You are the next chapter of that story.

You are now part of The Dentist's Tax Truths.

ABOUT THE FOUNDER

My name is Norman Dotch, RIA, and I am the CEO and Founder of The Dentist's Tax & Business Architecture System, R.O.B.S., Corporation. I am a native Spanish speaker from Panama. As a Tax Law Expert Architect and Registered Investment Advisor (RIA), **THE HIGHEST LEVEL OF LINCENSING**, I specialize in helping dentists with complex tax planning strategies and wealth management with the goal to protect up to 100% of their taxable income. With over two decades of experience in tax law and financial advising (**I have my Securities Licenses –Series 7 & 66 and Insurance License**), I focus on creating Tax Risk Assessments and Tax Plans by leveraging advanced tax strategies derived directly from the IRS tax codes, sections, regulations, losses, exclusions, and credits.

I understand the unique financial and life challenges dentists face and work closely with each client to develop customized strategies that not only reduce tax burdens but also support long-term financial growth. My approach combines tax savings with a comprehensive financial plan, ensuring that my clients can build a secure financial future, free from the stress of tax uncertainty.

www.ingramcontent.com/pod-product-compliance
Lightning Source LLC
LaVergne TN
LVHW050939210926
848482LV00013B/666